THE IMMIGRANTS' SON: A BRONX BOY'S STORY

How a child of Jewish immigrants became a high school sports star, family man and business executive amid personal challenges and struggles.

BY ARTHUR FRIEDMAN

The Immigrants' Son:
A Bronx Boy's Story
ISBN: 979-8-218-22318-2
Copyright © 2023 by Arthur Friedman.

For more information, email Arthur Friedman at:
artdart@optonline.com

Cover art by Karen Friedman
Book design by Sherry Wachter
Editing and production by Patrick Dunphy

Cataloging-in Publication Data

Friedman, Arthur
The Immigrants' Son: A Bronx Boy's story
How a child of Jewish immigrants became a high school sports star, family man and business executive amid personal challenges and struggles

p. cm.   ISBN 979-8-218-22318-2

1. Arthur Friedman—memoir 2. Jewish Family Life—20th Century 3. Immigrants—American experience 4. Coming of age—Bronx, New York 5. First Generation—American

E 184 J5 F795 2023   974.700 FR

Printed in the United States of America

CONTENTS

PREFACE

My father, Paul Friedman, loved to tell stories.

Most of them were about his time growing up in the Bronx in a large, complicated Jewish family during the Great Depression and World War II.

We all heard them – my sister Mona and I, his nieces and nephews, friends, coworkers or anyone who would listen. Mona would usually laugh at them or roll her eyes, but I was more intrigued as to what caused my father to do some of the things he did, how they turned out and what the ramifications were.

Maybe it was my innate curiosity that later led to me becoming a journalist and history professor. Perhaps it was the thought that a generation earlier some of these things could have happened to me. However, that is doubtful, since I grew up in different times to different parents in a different socioeconomic situation.

I wasn't the youngest of six siblings born to immigrant parents trying to assimilate to a new society in extremely trying times, as was my father. My mother, Claire, was warm and coddling, with an empathetic and sympathetic personality that came to be admired by many. My father wasn't a struggling tailor with a lack of education like his father was, but a successful businessman with a strong charitable mindset.

The sports connection and inheritance that Dad and I had were also the reason I was the recipient of more of his stories. These were triggered by events such as the annual New York Yankees Old Timer's Game, where he would try to name who was being announced as quickly as possible before announcers like Mel Allen, Frank Messer, John Sterling or Michael Kay said which Yankees great it was, a penchant for which I joined in and then took over.

There were also historical and political remembrances that Dad would discuss that most interested me, especially as I grew older and became interested in history and politics. These ran from the 1940s and 1950s periods that he recalled, to family vacations and visits to certain cities and sites that brought out memories and commentary.

The stories and memories in this book are as truthful as can be, given that Paul Friedman passed away more than 25 years ago at its writing. They are not meant to embarrass or denigrate anyone, but to portray a man's life as honestly as possible, with some indulgences for fullness and connectivity.

I never wrote down Dad's stories until this writing but committed them to memory and family lore. My remembrances were based on repetitiveness, some confirmation from other family members over the years, a bit of research, my own involvement in some incidents and the confidence that whatever holes I filled in came from logical conclusions, most likely scenarios and internal hunches.

I wanted to tell Dad's life story because I thought it represented a time capsule of sorts to people of comparable backgrounds who grew up in similar times. It's a story of how a man overcame many obstacles, from poverty to his family's emotional instability, to succeed in reaching certain levels of achievement and standing in society.

I also thought it was a fun story to tell that might amuse or inspire those who read it. As a journalist, I always felt that everybody had a story to tell of how they got where they were at a certain point in their lives. My favorite was that of the then-100-year-old Abe Schrader, who escaped the Holocaust, became a highly successful businessman, befriended presidents and mayors, and left a much larger imprint on the world than his small place in history will tell.

I have that same feeling about Paul Friedman, who mixed bravado with insecurity, talent with guile, and love with anger to become a singularly unique person who influenced some like me and his grandson, Andrew, and lies deep in the memories of those still around to remember him, like Joyce and Elliot, Don and Carol, Richard and Dvorah, Heath and Arnie. And of course, all his grandchildren.

This book is also a sequel of sorts to *To Break the Barrier* (Expedition Press, New York), written by Dad's uncle and my great uncle, Theodore Kleiner. Uncle Teddy's book was dedicated to his father, Israel Kleiner, a freedom fighter for Poland against Russia in 1863. Israel Kleiner was born in Tarnow, Poland in 1839 and became the father of 20 children, and as Uncle Teddy wrote in his book, "an unbelievable number of grandchildren, including my father, great-grandchildren, including me, and great-grandchildren," and yes, now great-great-grandchildren.

Published in 1962, Teddy Kleiner gave my father a signed copy in which he noted that the name of two of the main characters, one who represented his father, and one his father's grandson, as was my father, was named Paul, even more inspiration for me in writing this book. Israel Kleiner died in the city of his birth in 1937, 10 years after my father was born, at the age of 97. Family lore says he fathered his last child, which could have been my great aunt Dora, when he was 89 years old.

As Uncle Teddy wrote, his funeral was attended by representatives of the Polish government and patriotic societies, who gave him a "hero's burial...All honors were his at last, never to be taken away from him. It was his colorful life that inspired me to write this novel," Teddy said in his dedication.

Teddy wrote about how his father "broke the barrier" rarely done in his times and intermarried with an Italian Catholic woman, Fay Bendit, and had five children together: Teddy, Leah, Monya, Sadie and Dora. This bold and controversial act would play out later in Dad's life and become an emotional crisis for him to overcome more than once in his life, several decades apart.

While Dad and I had our moments and, in fact, some long periods of disharmony, we also had a very close bond built though living together, taking family vacations, praying side by side in the synagogue, cheering for our teams, and being father and son. While he sometimes made it difficult given his own challenges and shortcomings, his plusses outweighed his minuses to make him a role model to me.

Here's his story told through my eyes and heart.

STICKBALL AND CHICKEN SOUP

"Pinny, stand look-out for us!"

"No, I want to play! I can hit the ball farther than you guys!"

Pinny was Paul Friedman, also known as Pinya, later Pinhead or Paulie, an eight-year-old skinny kid from the Bronx, standing a couple of blocks away from the Grand Concourse, then considered the Park or Madison Avenue of the borough. He was a curly-haired Jewish boy, the youngest of six children of Aaron and Monya Friedman, "apparent" Polish and Russian immigrants.

Their country of origin isn't clear, thus the "apparent" status that was never quite exactly known but was explained and explored later to have possibly been Italian and German, respectively. This was not unusual for Jewish immigrants of the time – the period just prior to World War I. Records and memories indicate that the conditions of Jewish families during the era were like gypsies, roaming from one pogrom, disenfranchised or exiled village, city and country to another while maintaining their cultural heritage.

As noted in the Preface, Paul's "Uncle Teddy," Theodore Kleiner, wrote a book called *To Break the Barrier.* It essentially was about his father, Israel Kleiner, a freedom fighter for Poland in the late 1800s. Kleiner's second wife was an Italian woman, a non-Jew named Fay Bendit.

Kleiner's book, in which his father, Israel, was ironically or fatalistically given the name Paul, was mainly focused on the then-groundbreaking act of marrying out of the faith, and the ramifications and complexities it brought to him and his family.

Monya, who emigrated from Poland, was said to have been born to Israel and Fay, which was often disputed over the years by family members but confirmed by *Ancestry,* making her a half-Italian Catholic and half-Ashkenazi Jew. Aaron Friedman, for whom less history was passed down through the family or able to be confirmed by documentation through *Ancestry,* emigrated from Russia.

However, as the story goes, when Aaron, with his Hebrew name that did not need to be Anglicized, came to speak to immigration officials, either at Ellis Island in New York or the Port of Baltimore, he was supposedly asked "What is your name?"

Speaking little English, he was said to have thought he was being asked "What are you?" To this he was said to have replied, translated from Yiddish, "I am a free man," celebrating and denoting his coming to America and escaping religious persecution. So, the immigration official wrote down his name as Aaron Friedman and that became the family moniker.

Uncle Teddy said his real surname was Beckman, likely of German origin. This hasn't been confirmed, but Friedman seems quite fitting and has certainly stuck.

This history would help determine Paul's personality, predilections and life choices, but wouldn't completely define him, since his life also became one of a self-made man, successful in family and business.

He was also someone troubled by his upbringing. A child of uneducated parents who barely spoke English, he and his brothers and sisters all became quite assimilated, lost any Yiddish accent they heard at their small Bronx apartment or at synagogue, and went on to live their own versions of the American Dream.

Paul's persona was certainly influenced by his love of sports. He played varsity baseball and basketball at Monroe High School and was a lifelong New York Yankees fan. Later in life he became an avid New York Knicks, Rangers, and Giants fan as well—and that was it; no crossover fandom for him.

It's not clear who told Paul—or Pinny—to "stand watch" for the cops that day the boys were playing stickball in the street, but it was clear why. Playing the game was forbidden in the busy Bronx streets of 1935. The older kids had occupied the park, and playing in the streets kept the younger kids within eye and earshot of their mothers' calls for dinner.

It might have come from Paul's nearest brother in age, Sam, or some other boy from the neighborhood just a couple of years older than him. Pinny had one other brother, Morris, the oldest in the family who emigrated with the oldest sister, Fay, and two other sisters, Ruthie and Francis, who like Paul and Sam, were born in the Bronx.

Pinny did play "watch out" for a while, but when one of the boys were called home by a yell from up the block, the other boys said, "Come on Pinny, you can play."

With television not yet invented, Paul gravitated to baseball, or in this case stickball, by necessity, purely by influence, listening to an occasional game on the radio, reading about it in the newspaper or hearing about it on the streets or in school.

Either way, he was an early natural with innate athletic ability and a competitiveness not unusual in the crowded and intense inner-city environment during the Great Depression. Soon, he would latch on to idolatry of Joe DiMaggio and love of the Yankees, and he certainly already knew about Babe Ruth and Lou Gehrig, but for now it was something ingrained in his early psyche.

There were no gloves used to play stickball, nor any bases, just markers on the street, and the bat was a broom stick "borrowed" from someone's mother or "found" on the street. The ball was a Spalding bought at the store for 2 cents that someone scrounged up or had given to them by a generous older sibling. The ball, also used for curb ball and stoop ball, was precious and had to be kept from going into the sewer.

Base hits were determined by how far the ball was hit. A single could be the end of the first building, a double the second sewer, a triple the corner light post and a homer the third sewer. A foul ball only occurred when the ball was interfered with by someone on the street or was otherwise unretrievable. Balls hit off the building were playable and if someone broke a window, all players ran like hell.

So, Pinny got up to bat, swung and missed in the first pitch, hit a double his second time up and smashed a homer before Monya called him in to dinner. He was mostly a happy kid, eating his chicken soup that filled the room with its iconic odor, some *challah* bread and a piece of *mandel* bread for his meal.

The family was poor, stuck in the throes of the Depression like the rest of the country, but Jewish families always found a way to eat. Being poor meant struggling to make ends meet, but the condition of poverty didn't really exist for most Jews.

Families shared, houses of worship did what they could to provide sustenance, especially during the Sabbath, and older children took jobs as soon as they could. This didn't mean forgoing school at any level because even these Jews who emigrated from *shtetels* knew from their heritage and upbringing the value and importance of being learned, whether that was from *Torah* studies and their new American public schools.

Around the table was Paul's father, Aaron, a tailor who found little work during the tough times, but found some, and still played cards with his friends and minded that the *kindelah,* or children, be taken care of. Monya, who some called the Anglicized Mary, was a simple woman who liked to cook, with mediocre aplomb, and baked with slightly more success, but doted over all her children. She took in the clothes of the more well-to-do to wash in order to make some money and kept in touch with her many relatives who often came by to visit over a *glezel tei,* or cup of tea.

Paul's eldest siblings, Morris and Fay, were already out of the house and married. Francis, 10 years older than him, was finishing high school and Ruthie was a young, rebellious 16-year-old, while Sam was just two years older than Pinny, allowing them to share some friends and activities like going to Sunday and Hebrew School.

On the surface, they seemed like the typical Jewish family of the times, but problems and circumstances would arise that were at once endemic of the period and somewhat unique to the personalities of all involved, especially the parents.

Clearly, assimilation played a large role in how the family struggled to fit into society and its customs, mores and prejudices. Perhaps it was Monya and her siblings' upbringing that saw them seek refuge from a Europe that was being pulled in many directions, or maybe it was their status as children of an intermarriage.

Aaron's background is more unknown, but family stories made clear that he was a troubled man from an insecure past who brought mental instability and an irritable nature to the family and his children.

One aspect of the Friedman family that became apparent surely had its origins in those early days – a sense of jealousy and envy of others with more education and financial means. This manifested itself in a yearning to succeed and improve their status. However, it also imparted a negative underlying sense of guilt in Aaron and Monya's children, who'd had it easier than them.

This led to sibling feuding and guilt trips often spurred by Monya's inane comments like who was the prettiest granddaughter or who gave her more money.

MINE BABY

When Pinny was 10, some patterns began to emerge that would become an integral part of what gave him, as many would later claim, "a large personality."

It was also when he started to become wildly interested in sports, a fanatic. He would grow to love the competition, the athleticism, the grace, the level playing field, the celebrity and the loyalty that sports created and nurtured.

This love of sports started with baseball and the New York Yankees playing down the street from where Pinny lived. He would hear about them from older boys and the fame of Babe Ruth and Lou Gehrig. He would also learn about Hank Greenberg, also known as "Hammerin' Hank" or "The Hebrew Hammer," a Jewish ballplayer for the American League rival Detroit Tigers, from the radio and newspapers.

Somehow, Pinny got it in his head that he wanted, needed, to go to a Yankees game. On Sunday, May 8, 1938, Paul, who wouldn't turn 11 until July, decided he was going to the game. He didn't know how he was going to get in, since he didn't have the money, nor did he know what the ramifications would be because he thought his parents would just think he was out playing with his friends.

So, after Sunday School on the cool early spring day, he got home, put on his jacket, and said, "Mom, I'm going to watch a ballgame at the park," which in essence was true but in reality would not have been allowed.

As Paul said years later, "I really didn't think it out. In my mind, I could just go to the game, figure out how to get in and be home before anyone noticed." Monya said, "All right Pinya, but you stay close to home and don't be out too long."

Pinny started walking to the park, then veered off down Jerome Avenue toward Yankee Stadium. He started thinking about his favorite player, the young star Joe DiMaggio, who had sprung onto the scene two years earlier and fit right in with the Bronx Bombers and the likes of Lou Gehrig, Bill Dickey and Charlie Keller.

As he got closer to the ballpark, Paul began thinking about how he was going to get in. Standing off near the main gate on 161st Street, he noticed all the men were wearing long coats under their suits, as was the normal attire in those days. He saw one young boy and his dad enter the gate and it appeared like the boy, who was cold and probably a little scared of the crowds, was grabbing onto his father's leg so tight that he was inside his coat.

In maybe the first instance of his future nickname later given to him by his mother-in-law, Bessie Schwartz, for his unorthodox way of playing Gin Rummy, "Pinya the Bluffer" sidled his way up to an older man wearing an unbuttoned long coat swaying in the brisk breeze, and ducked between the coat and the man's leg just as they entered the gate. Security not being anywhere near the level it became decades later, Paul made it through without being seen and then quickly walked away. The man in the long coat who had provided him concealment gave him no notice.

He was in. Now, Pinny saw a nearby walkway to the stands. He made his way in as the Yankees and Chicago White Sox were finishing up hitting and fielding practice. He was amazed at the size of the stadium, the field, the players and the crowd. He was one of 28,440 people at the game and for one of the few times in his life, was left speechless.

Paul decided he would sit near a family and found a spot a few seats away from a father and two sons. Nobody ever checked his ticket, as the stadium was just about half full and again security was lax.

It was also Paul's forming personality that gave him the confidence or courage, like he was to tell his son years later, "If you walk in like you own the place, like you belong, often people will take no notice that maybe you don't."

Pinny's eyes and ears were wide open to the sights and sounds he was witnessing. The huge, awe-inspiring Yankee Stadium, with the green grass seeming to sparkle, with the players larger than can be imagined, the pinstriped uniforms dazzling in their regal manner. Though Pinny rose in excitement when Joe DiMaggio strode up to bat, his child's stature meant that no one shouted, "Down in front."

The game turned out to be amazing. Lou Gehrig hit a two-run home run in the fourth inning, and Tommy Henrich and DiMaggio hit back-to-back solo home runs in the sixth. Red Ruffing pitched a complete game and the Yankees won 7-3. The game only took an hour and 54 minutes, but during that time, trouble was brewing back home.

Shortly after Paul made his way to the ballpark, his Aunt Sadie and cousins Thelma and Florence came in from Rockaway by subway to visit and do a little shopping on the Grand Concourse. Pinny either wasn't aware they were coming or had forgotten.

Naturally, Monya wanted her children to say hello to the visiting relatives and went to gather them up. She quickly found Francis, Ruthie and Sammy, but Paul wasn't at the park and Sammy didn't know where he was.

"*Pinya, vas makhstu* (where are you)?" she shouted down the street several times.

She sent Sammy to find Aaron next door playing cards with his friends and told him Monya wanted him. This would have irritated him, no doubt, being an irritable man to begin with and not liking being taken from his card game or his *kibbitzing.*

The relatives had left and would come back later, but the other children were there in the apartment and Monya was crying. "Pinya is missing. I can't find him," she said.

They sent Sammy back to the park for another look and Ruthie and Francis around the neighborhood to search for him. Aaron and Monya went out on the sidewalk in front of the apartment to keep look out. They were frightened, upset and angry, especially the short-tempered Aaron, who was becoming furious.

The siblings came back without word and Aaron questioned Sammy if he really didn't know where Pinya was. He said he didn't, either because he really didn't know or didn't want to snitch on his brother or feel his father's wrath.

As they were looking one way up the street, Pinny started coming toward them. He quickly realized that, while he thought he wouldn't be missed, he was now in trouble.

"*Mein God, vu bistu geven* (my God, where were you)?" Monya screamed.

"Come here right now, Pinya!" Aaron commanded.

"Oh no," Paul said to himself, and squeezed past his parents and ran upstairs to the apartment, into his bedroom and under his bed, now knowing he hadn't gotten away with his little field trip.

Aaron and Monya were truly frightened that something had happened to their youngest child, even though he had often been out of the house and their sight for several hours. Perhaps they had that parental sense that something was different this time, especially when he didn't respond to their calling for him on the street. Maybe it was Monya's disappointment that he wasn't there when Sadie, Thelma and Florence had come to visit.

For Paul, there was first confusion. Why were his parents so upset? He had been out of their sight before down at the park for a few hours just like now without any concern. Then there was fear of what kind of punishment he was about to receive, especially when he told them where he'd been, which he had to do.

When Aaron and Monya made their way upstairs they were both yelling: "Where were you and where are you?

"I was at the Yankees game," Pinya said from under the bed.

"What, you went to Yankee Stadium by yourself?" Monya asked.

"You're not allowed to go there by yourself and where did you get the money?" Aaron asked.

"I didn't know I wasn't allowed, and I snuck in," said Pinya, now crying his eyes out, still under the bed's big back springs.

"Get out from under that bed Pinchus, I want to speak to you!" Aaron exclaimed.

"No, you're going to hit me and I didn't do anything wrong," Pinya said.

At that point Aaron, infuriated, reached under the bed to grab his son and let out a loud *gishrei* (yell) – he had caught his arm on a jagged spring and was badly hurt.

He pulled his arm out from under the bed and was bleeding with a scrape from under his elbow to his wrist. Monya screamed and got a towel to wrap around the wound. At that point Francis, Ruthie, Florence and Thelma came rushing upstairs to see what was going on.

"He has to go to the hospital," Francis said. "I'll go with you. Can you all get Pinny out from under the bed and stay with him?"

"Yes, we can," they said. "Just go!"

While Aaron, Monya and Francis left the apartment headed to the emergency room, Ruthie tried to coax Paul out from under the bed.

"I don't know why you went to that game, Pinny, but you have to get out from under there before you get hurt," his sister said. "Let me talk to you, silly boy. It's going to be alright but come out from there."

His cousins echoed similar thoughts and Pinny slowly crawled out from deep under the bed, crying and afraid. Accepting Ruthie's appeal to come hug her on top of the bed, Paul wept: "Is Poppa going to be OK? I didn't kill him, did I?"

Ruthie, Florence and Thelma giggled a bit and comforted him that, no, that didn't happen.

"He's going to get stitched up and be home soon, I'm sure," Ruthie said. "The real question is, 'What in the world were you doing, going to that ball game all by yourself?' That's not smart or safe Pinny. You had us all very scared."

"I didn't think anyone would notice I was missing," he said, calming down a bit. "When I go to the park or play on the street Momma and Poppa aren't scared where I am. I just didn't think it was such a bad thing to do. I'm sorry. I hope Poppa is OK."

"Yes, but when they sent Sammy to get you and you weren't there, that was bad and scary," Ruthie said.

Speaking of Sammy, he suddenly appeared at the doorway of the room.

"So, there you are," Ruthie exclaimed. "I was starting to get worried about you, too. What happened to you?"

"I was just downstairs on the stoop trying to stay out of trouble," Sammy said. "I saw them leave for the hospital and Francis said to go upstairs so here I am. Is everything OK?"

"Yes, I think so," Ruthie said. "Stay with your brother a minute. Thelma and Florence have to get going."

The cousins hugged Paul and comforted him, did the same to Sammy, and then walked out of the bedroom with Ruthie, headed back to Rockaway.

Sammy jumped up on the bed next to Paul, half hugged and elbowed him, and said, "What a dope. If you had told me where you were going, I could have covered for you. It'll be alright. When they get home, Mom and Pop will probably be so tired and relieved that all is OK, you might not even get punished."

"All OK in here," Ruthie said upon returning to the room.

"I'm hungry and thirsty," Pinny said.

"Ok, let's go get you some milk and cookies," Ruthie responded.

A couple of hours later, the three siblings sitting in the living room, Francis, Monya and Aaron walked back in the front door, Aaron's arm bandaged up but some calm seeming to come over them all.

"What happened at the hospital?" asked Ruthie, who would become a nurse in a few years.

"It was just a bad scratch, not too deep, and they just bandaged him up and gave him some ointment and aspirin to take," Francis said. "He's OK."

Pinny got up and slowly walked toward him father.

"I'm sorry Poppa," he said. "I didn't mean to scare anybody. I won't do it again. I'm glad you're not hurt too bad."

Monya told Aaron to go sit down and got him some *mandel* bread and some Schnapps. After a snort, Aaron told his son, "Pinny, that was bad what you did going to that stupid game and then hiding from me. I hope you learned a lesson about what you did. Come give me and your mother a hug."

Paul dutifully did just that, still not convinced he did anything wrong, but sorry his father got hurt and that he got in trouble. It would be a few years before he saw another Yankees game. Man did he love that team and baseball!

And Sammy was correct. Paul had to stay inside for a few days after school, but Monya wasn't much on discipline – she yelled a lot, but not much else – and Aaron really couldn't be bothered with the role of fatherhood. He could be strict and even irrational, but he'd rather spend time playing cards and going to synagogue then teach his children life lessons.

Pinny did not really get in trouble for his day at "The Park that Ruth Built," and he got to see Joe DiMaggio hit a homerun! The Yankees and sports were in his blood. He satisfied his growing desire for competition and physical exertion. Later, that desire to compete, to stretch himself, helped him succeed in a world where a young Jewish boy faced many hurdles.

Monya and Aaron Friedman, around 1945

Arthur Friedman

SAY KADDISH

Pinny had an unusual, often strained relationship with his family. He was 17 years younger than his oldest brother, Morris, and 15 years younger than his oldest sister, Faye. So, by the time Paul could remember, they were both out of the house. While he saw them often for family holidays and in Faye's case, visits, they were more like close cousins than a typical sibling relationship.

Paul's parents did not assimilate too quickly or well into the American society to which they had immigrated. Certainly not as well as some of his aunts and uncles, or his future in-laws, Joseph and Bessie Schwartz.

Aaron was what was considered "learned" in the *Torah* meaning he studied it and knew its verses and meanings, but not much else. He was a tailor by trade, but didn't seem to work much, especially during the Depression, and had a temper that he used as a way to discipline his children rather than by example or life lessons. According to Paul, he reveled during Passover Seders, singing the traditional songs long into the night.

Mary was a simple housewife who showed love and attention to her children, but nothing too deep. The one thing they apparently did instill was the importance of education and for people making a place for themselves in society. All the children graduated from high school, and most, if not all achieved some level of college or adult education.

Morris became a textile executive, a political activist who even dabbled in the early days of Communism and was an avid writer. Faye worked in offices doing clerical work and was a loving wife and mother.

Pinny was closest to his younger sisters, Francis and Ruthie, even though they were ten and eight years older than him, and his brother Sam, just two years older. Francis was very much a mother figure, helping Paul with schoolwork and the ways of life, while Ruthie was kind of a wild child but close to her brothers nonetheless.

Before Paul could remember, Faye married a young local boy named Joseph Gabamonte, an Italian deliveryman and driver who the family had known from the neighborhood and was well-liked by all. Perhaps it was this familiarity and his low-key nature that caused no problems when he married Faye even though he was a non-Jew, a *goy*.

The same was not true, Paul was to find out just a few months removed from his Yankee Stadium adventure, when it came to Ruthie. Asleep one morning because it was either a holiday or too early for temple or Sunday School or perhaps it was late that summer, Pinny was startled awake by his father.

"Pinya, get up," Aaron said in Yiddish. "You are coming with me to say *Kaddish*. Your sister, Ruth, is dead!"

A wave of fear, sadness and shock overcame the young boy. *What?* he thought. *I love Ruthie! She can't be dead. I just saw her yesterday.* He knew *Kaddish* was a prayer people said when someone died, but he had never said it.

"Come, we're going to temple to say *Kaddish* for Ruthie," Aaron insisted.

The rest was fuzzy for Paul to remember, in great part because he didn't recall this incident until about 35 years later. This occurred while he was in therapy after suffering a nervous breakdown and depression caused, the doctor said, by overwork, a high-pressure job, and repressing traumatic events like this.

It's hard to imagine a worse way to tell a 10-year-old child that his sister was dead. It's worse still when she wasn't.

Ruthie was quite alive and would be for decades to come. What she had done was marry a non-Jewish man, one Aaron apparently found far less acceptable than Joe Gabamonte. Richard Pinkowitz, Francis's son, said years later that the hypocrisy "was unbelievable and ruined, or at least damaged lives," for no good reason.

If Aaron had been strict in his belief that Jewish women should only marry in the faith, it would have been one obstacle for the family to overcome. The fact that it was hypocritical toward one daughter and not the other made it worse.

To involve a 10-year-old son and brother is nothing less than cruel and leans toward insanity. As Richard said more than once, "If you grew up a Friedman and you were able to keep your sanity, it's an accomplishment."

When Paul did remember the traumatic occurrence, he thought that he never actually said *Kaddish,* and that either his mother or Francis had stepped in and stopped his father from forcing him to partake in the horror. It was also likely to him that they had cleared the air about Ruthie.

She had apparently eloped with a man unknown to the family, not Jewish and possibly not white. What happened after that was also unclear, but the marriage was evidently annulled, and Ruth was forced into an arranged marriage with an older Jewish man named Max Brownstein, with whom she had a decent but unloving relationship for many years.

The effect on Paul was profound and psychologically damaging. The impact on Ruth was real and raw. She led a fairly good life, moving to Jacksonville, Florida, and becoming a nurse. She never had children and never quite seemed happy, although she always loved her little brother Paul.

Ruthie stayed close to her mother – Aaron died in 1952 – but there was always something off or missing about her. There was sadness and irrational behavior that simmered throughout her life.

At one point, Ruthie said she wanted to take care of her mother and the family arranged for Monya to live in a nursing home near where Ruthie lived. The family – mainly Sam and Paul – sent money to Ruthie to fund that arrangement, which she apparently mismanaged or misappropriated. Dad and I had to finally fly down to Florida and take my grandmother home to live with us at first, and then at a nursing home near our house.

This was traumatic for me and Dad, since Ruthie had never seemed mean-spirited, especially toward her mother. But who knows what feelings or incidences she was repressing. After all, there was her annulled marriage and subsequent fixed and loveless marriage for which her mother was a participant.

For Paul, the incident left scars and did teach him some life lessons that he would use to his benefit later on. For now, there was a youngster who needed to grow into a man, and he would soon meet someone who changed his life forever.

CLAIRE SCHWARTZ

Paul had just had his bar mitzvah, a low-key, low-budget affair in the synagogue, which was typical for the poor Jews in the Bronx in 1940. He would later be accustomed to more lavish affairs he threw for his son's bar mitzvah or his daughter's wedding.

Pinny was getting taller and more muscular, which only fed his growing love of competing in sports of all kinds. He played baseball in Crotona Park whenever he could and had also started playing a lot of basketball. He was thirteen, athletic and outgoing, and began to be increasingly interested in girls.

One day down at the park, a friend of Paul's introduced him to a girl she knew from her synagogue who lived in a different neighborhood.

"Hey Paul, this is my friend Claire Schwartz," the young lady said. "Want to go get a chocolate soda with us?"

"Hi Claire. Sure, I'd love to go," said Pinny, who had some money on him from his bar mitzvah. "What brings you down to the park today?"

"Oh, my brother Robert was playing basketball with the older boys on the other court," said Claire, who was 12, petite in stature, but with a great smile and rather beautiful features, Pinny thought. "He's going to CCNY next year to play ball. But he's going to be a scientist."

Robert Schwartz would indeed go on to play basketball at City College under the great Nat Holman. He would also go on to be a renowned scientist, inventing the atomic cannon, which meant a small atomic bomb could be used with a battlefield cannon.

Robert drew up the plans for the atomic cannon sitting alone in a small office – he called it a closet – at Picatinny Arsenal in Dover, N.J. It gave the United States a tactical advantage in the brewing Cold War and added to the capabilities of the U.S. army at the early stages of the Korean War. It was never used, which under the theory of nuclear deterrence was the point. Robert received the U.S. Medal of Honor for his invention.

At the soda shop, Claire actually ordered an egg cream, which was and would be her favorite drink for her whole life. Paul stuck with the chocolate soda and couldn't keep his eyes off Claire.

"Man, she is pretty," he said to himself. "I'd like to see her again."

Pinny did find ways to run into Claire over the next few months. One day, he asked her if she wanted to go to the park with him and then get an ice cream. Claire said she would have to ask her parents, Joseph and Bessie, who said it was OK as long as her sister Helen, who had just turned eighteen, would chaperone.

Helen came along, which made Pinny nervous. And when he was nervous, he tended to be a bit of a wise guy, making stupid jokes and saying some awkward things. Claire thought he was funny and handsome, but Helen wasn't taken by his wisecracks.

"He's kind of a wise guy," Helen would tell Claire later. "But he is kind of good-looking and he definitely likes you."

"All the boys are like that," said the now-14-year-old Claire. "I think you made him nervous. And I think I like him, too."

The childish flirtatiousness would continue for the next year or so. One day, Claire asked her parents if she could invite Paul over for Shabbat dinner on Friday night.

"Whatever your mother wants," Joe said.

"Of course, you can," said Bessie, always wanting to show off her cooking and make Claire happy.

At that point, Claire, who had skipped eighth grade based on her perfect grades and teachers' recommendations, was about to enter Taft High School, while Paul would be attending Monroe High School and was looking forward to playing organized sports for the first time.

The dinner went well. Pinny was on his best behavior and absolutely loved Bessie's cooking. Claire giggled at how much chicken soup, brisket and potatoes he ate and how he loved the apple strudel he devoured for dessert.

Joe appreciated his well-behaved manner, his ability to speak some Yiddish and that he seemed like a "good Jewish boy." Bessie thought the same, loved how he praised her food, and how he looked at and behaved toward Claire – playful but respectful.

While Joe went off to Friday night services, the three of them played some cards. That night might have been when Bessie dubbed Paul "Pinya the Bluffer," for his card playing strategy. Claire giggled when her mother said that and Paul bellowed his signature cackle laugh. It was a good night.

MONROE HIGH AND MARRIAGE

Paul and Claire began dating as would have been expected for teenagers of the time. They took walks in Crotona Park, watched ball games being played and went to matinee movies.

Pinny would also take any opportunity he could to eat lunch or dinner at the Schwartz house whenever he could. It gave him a chance to see Claire and enjoy Bessie's cooking, which he loved.

The thing is, as Paul would express many times later in life, not only was his mother not the greatest cook – baking was more her thing – but Bessie was a great cook, from matzo ball soup and stuffed cabbage to pot roast and brisket.

He also realized early on and became entranced over the specialness of Claire. First, she was a cute girl and was becoming a beautiful woman, with her high cheekbones, sweet smile, warm laugh and soulful eyes. Second, she was smart, leaning toward brilliant. She had already skipped eighth grade and would soon skip 10th, graduating Taft High School at age 16 with perfect grades.

But more than that, Claire had a great ability for empathy and sympathy toward others. She was able to feel and soothe the pain or sorrow of others with her words and deeds without making it seem like she was burdened or going out of her way. This was important to Paul, who needed nurturing, caring and love, for he came from a household that had little of any of this, his mother unable to express or understand a child's problems and his father not caring or unable to bother.

Claire adored and fawned over her parents, with a mother-daughter bond with Bessie that was deep and a deeply respectful and playful relationship with Joseph that broke down his often-dour demeanor.

As the youngest of five siblings, she was also everybody's baby sister who was wise beyond her years. Harold and Robert were protective of her and as she got older realized they could rely on her for insight and warmth maybe not expected from a younger sister.

Sophie, 12 years older, was a close older sister and surrogate mother in that she introduced Claire to the ways of the times in America as she grew that sometimes her immigrant parents could not. Helen, four years older, was her buddy and confidant – they looked alike, talked alike and built a special friendship that only sisters can have.

By the time they were in high school, Paul and Claire grew inseparable. For Paul, she was perfect in every way, a feeling he kept his entire life. She had the outer and inner beauty that was magnetic to him, and the caring and nurturing ability he so desired and needed.

For Claire, Paul's outgoing and verbose personality helped overcome her shyness and bring out her special nature. He was also handsome, athletic and kindhearted in his own way.

Paul also showed Claire's parents and brother and sisters respect and friendship that mattered to Claire and was a portent of a future in which Paul would have a closer relationship to Claire's family than to his own.

Claire was also to spend much time watching and cheering Pinny on in sports, since as he entered high school, he was able to play organized athletics and be on organized teams for the first time. Paul played baseball and basketball and ran track at Monroe High School, excelling particularly in baseball and basketball.

Naturally, as he became entrenched in sports, he also made strong friendships, notably with Sammy Tolkoff and Jonesy. As their friendships grew, so did Claire grow close to them and their girlfriends like Sam's bride-to-be, Eleanor. Of course, as Paul and Sammy became the top two athletes in the school, they also became rivals, but in a friendly way.

Claire, being who she was, would come to games and cheer them both on, and Paul would tease her not to cheer more for Sammy than for him.

"I would say 'he already has a big enough head, don't make it bigger,'" Paul would recall later. Claire would just laugh and continue doing what she was doing, knowing he could have also been talking about himself.

By the time Paul was a junior at Monroe, he was a star athlete along with Sammy Tolkoff. Paul played centerfield like his hero, Joe DiMaggio, and forward on the basketball team.

Sammy also had great abilities, Paul would proudly recall, and also the charisma to be a leader on and off the field or court. When Sammy talked, people listened, they laughed and they wanted to follow him.

Pinny suffered a difficult loss in the New York City High School basketball finals, when, after hitting a late basket to give Monroe the lead, the future Hall of Famer Dolph Shayes took a shot at halfcourt that banked in to win the game and the city championship. Monroe was shocked and disappointed, and Pinny cried his eyes out, only to be quickly comforted by Claire.

At the end of their senior year, it was heartbreaking when the star varsity players and best friends knew only one of them would be named athlete of the year. Paul, not a great student, was more well-rounded and might have had a statistical edge, or maybe the coaches thought he was more humble than Sammy.

Whatever the reason, at the end of year awards dinner, Paul was named Athlete of the Year. Now it was Sammy's turn to cry.

Paul was to say years later that he thought Sammy deserved it and maybe more than that, that he really wanted it. So, at his 50th birthday party, it was Claire's idea to give Sammy the medal, much to my disappointment.

Sammy cried again, but he had already proven to be a lifelong friend who treated the Friedman family like VIPs when they came to Brown's hotel in the Catskills for many years. Sammy had become the Athletic Director at Brown's and embraced the Friedmans every time they came with special treatment and became an uncle and mentor to me.

The original "Mr. T," Sammy became the high school basketball and baseball coach at Monroe for 35 years and was an assistant basketball coach at Fordham University. As the *New York Post* wrote when Sam died, "He may have outlived his fame, but for over 70 years Tolkoff cast a giant shadow."

Meanwhile, Claire graduated Taft High School at age 16 and started Hunter College as a chemistry major. She was doing great until the horrible day when she saw someone pushed in front of the subway train on her way to school. She never rode the subway again, and had to withdraw from school. There's no telling where her career would have led, but Claire was ready to go on with her life, pursuing other rewards and endeavors.

When Paul graduated Monroe, he began a 45-year career in the apparel industry. He got a job at Curtis Stores Inc. in the Bronx as a merchandise assistant working for Irving Schneider, who became a mentor and career booster, with Paul working for him for the next 25 years.

Schneider paid for Paul to attend McDowell's Fashion School of Patternmaking in Manhattan, where he learned apparel manufacturing, and most importantly for his career, store and window display and merchandising. He was soon to become a buyer for Curtis Stores.

Meanwhile, Paul and Claire were clearly in love and wanted to get married. Joe and Bessie thought that was great, but Claire was still 17 and the parents said they needed to wait until Claire was the legal age of 18. So, they did.

One month after Claire turned 18, she married Paul on Dec. 14, 1946, a marriage that would last 51 years. As it is said, "For better or for worse, for richer or poorer, in sickness and in health, they loved and cherished each other every day of their life."

Paul, Mona and Claire Friedman 1953

Arthur Friedman

A FAMILY AND A CAREER BLOSSOM

Pinny worked hard and Claire worked part-time jobs and took care of their apartment in the Bronx for the next five years. On March 18,1951, they had their first child, a daughter they named Mona Carol, and the Hebrew *Malka Shayna,* meaning "beautiful queen."

Claire and Paul were in bliss over their darling daughter, who was embraced by all, especially Claire's family, who were so happy for their baby sister. While Paul continued to put in long hours, now there was greater cause and need.

And Claire had a wonderful support system in Bessie and Sophie, as grandmother and aunt of the vivacious, adorable Mona, a smart, inquisitive, wonderful child.

In 1955, Schneider closed the Curtis operation as the Bronx was changing socioeconomically and opened Great Eastern Department Stores on Route 17 in Paramus, N.J. Schneider brought Paul there as general merchandise manager (GMM).

Great Eastern, which eventually grew to six stores – five in New Jersey and one in New York – was one of the early large-scale regional discounters in the New York metropolitan area, similar to rivals Two Guys and Korvette's. Paul soon had offices in the Little Falls, N.J., store, and was travelling into New York City's Garment District often as a GMM.

That same year, Paul and Claire had their second child, Arthur Charles, on April 4. I was named after Aaron Friedman, who had died two years earlier at the age of 66, and Claire's grandfather, Chaim Schwartz. I was given the Hebrew name Aaron.

So, it became for years to come, during religious ceremonies and observances, that Paul was Pinchus *ben* (son of) Aaron and Arthur was Aaron *ben* Pinchus, which always gave Paul great *nachas* and joy, as it did our longtime rabbi when we moved to Clifton, N.J., Rabbi Eugene Markovitz.

I quickly was given the nickname Arty by my father and was generally known by that or Art by friends and family. We lived in the Bronx for two years before the family moved to a garden apartment in Bayside, Queens, as the Bronx neighborhood and Jewish community started to change in the post-World War II era.

While a couple of long-lasting friendships were made in the Bronx, the two-year stint in Bayside produced even longer-term relationships, particularly with the Frye and Crimi families. It also afforded the Friedmans a more suburban environment of grass and trees and playgrounds and common areas for community barbecues and neighborly outings, a lifestyle they would choose to follow for the rest of their lives.

In 1959, we moved to Clifton, N.J., a formerly rural but quickly growing northern New Jersey town that was becoming a sprawling suburban city. We lived on a street with a cul-de-sac that had friendly neighbors, mainly with children around the ages of Mona and me, and Claire's parents moved there with us to help pay the mortgage and move out of the Bronx.

The bottom floor and basement of 127 Huemmer Terrace were converted to living quarters for Joe and Bessie, with a living room, bedroom, full bath and kitchen. Joe was a retired tailor and brought with him a sewing machine that he proficiently used for helping the family repair clothes.

A proud member of the International Ladies Garment Workers Union, he would watch television, from the new Westerns that dominated the airwaves to the news in which he favored all Democrats like any good union man did, and cursed out Republicans – "Nixon, Rockefeller, Lindsay, they should all go in the hell," Joe often proclaimed, referring to the former vice president, New York governor and New York City mayor of the time, in his Yiddish accent.

Bessie died in 1963, while Joe lived until 1969, happily seeing his only grandson have his bar mitzvah and partaking in family vacations and parties.

Paul spent 15 years at Great Eastern, becoming a vice president. He flourished during his time both as a businessman and socially. His staff of buyers became his close friends, as well, with many weekend family outings with the likes of Norman, Howie and the rest, and he struck up one of his closest relationships with Danny Madison, who co-owned a hosiery company with Pat Dapalone.

Danny was a sweet talking, suave Madison Avenue type, and I always wondered if he just used his surname because it was so fitting. Danny hosted cocktail parties that Paul and Claire attended, and he and other "garmentos" regularly gave Paul tickets to New York Yankees, Knicks and Rangers

Paul Friedman - around 1975

games and Broadway shows as thanks for Paul buying their products for the Great Eastern chain.

This lifestyle suited Paul in so many ways. It quenched his thirst for sports, which he continued to love, lifted his ego left bereft by being the youngest of six siblings and the child of parents who knew nothing of psychology and gave him little attention or praise for any of his accomplishments.

While he was slowly making a better salary, it also let him live a bit above his means, not having to pay for the events he was attending, absorbing and loving. They were also an important release from the daily grind and pressures of the job. For while Schneider and his son, Mel, who had joined the business, were mentoring to Paul, they were also applying the usual pressure of profits and sales for which he was not the best equipped to handle mentally.

This often left Paul stressed out after a long day or week and it fell on Claire to be the sounding board of some late-night talks of frustration and an inability to handle the pressures and long hours. Dad's anger would sometimes put a strain on family life, but Mom kept the moments at bay, at least in those days, and we generally led an idyllic life.

Paul's access to great seats to these sporting events would soon also become his best way to bond with me. Around the age of six or seven, Dad started to take me to Yankees, Knicks and Rangers games and we had the greatest times.

Dad and I both drank in the charisma of Mickey Mantle, the skills of Whitey Ford and the aura of Yankee Stadium. Walking into Yankee Stadium and seeing the bright green field, the giant scoreboard and the sounds of the game – the smack of the bat hitting the ball during batting practice, the gloves hugging the balls with a pop during fielding practice and the voice of Bob Shepperd giving the starting lineup – sent tingles up Dad's and my spines.

We often attended these games with Harry Donenfeld, husband of Sophie and father of Felice. Uncle Harry was a complicated man. He wrote comedy books, did some radio in his younger days and became a tie and shirt salesman. However, he always seemed troubled and unhappy about the way his life turned out.

But Harry was also in his element at the game. His contribution was usually a big bag of peanuts that filled the car with its fresh odor when we picked him up in the Bronx north of the stadium before the game.

Harry enjoyed his brother-in-law Paul's company and personality, bellowing out cheers to his team and jeers to the opponents and umpires. Everyone always said Harry was nicer to me than his own daughter, inviting me to play catch outside when they visited our house, making funny noises and telling corny jokes. Felice often said, "You were the son he never had, and I wasn't."

Dad loved to tell stories and reminisce about Joe DiMaggio and the Yankees of the 1940s and fifties. We attended Rangers and Knicks games at the old Madison Square Garden on Eighth Avenue and West 48th Street in Manhattan, where if you had a bad seat behind a post, you spent the night straining to see the game. We never had those seats.

I remember asking why all the men were throwing their hats on the ice when Rod Gilbert scored his third goal of the game. Dad explained that it was called a hat trick and that it was a tradition to throw their hats on the ice. Paul never wore a hat because his head was too big, or as he said, "I have a Friedman head!"

I wasn't there when there was a typical Paul Friedman incident at a Rangers game a few years later. Evidently, there were two Boston Bruins fans at the game bullying and getting physical with a Rangers fan exiting the arena.

The way Dad relayed the story, he jumped in to rescue the Rangers fan, grabbing one bully and putting him in a headlock and throwing and landing a couple of solid punches

                                            Arthur Friedman

on the other guy. Garden security then got involved, and Dad said, "They were all stunned, and I just walked away."

When he got home, Mom scolded him for getting involved and putting himself at risk – he was in his forties by then and overweight, but his arms were still strong and his rage was still able to be called upon. For Paul, it was pure instinct that kicked in.

"I couldn't just do nothing, Claire," Paul said. "That wouldn't be right. I really didn't think, I just reacted."

It was as if the rough and tumble boy from the Bronx came out, the one that had an occasional street fight, who boldly snuck into Yankee stadium, who was the top athlete with a sense of right and justice, who knew Jews stood up for themselves and people stood up for each other when it was necessary because your own family or society might not or because you had the inner fortitude and physical attributes and the inner rage that allowed you to.

I was fairly speechless and proud and said something like, "You're a crazy animal," at which Dad just let out his signature cackle and hugged me. I think Mona was crying and laughing at the same time, as she was known to do, and Mom just hugged her and that was it.

Later, we had seats in the fourth row behind the basket when legendary Knicks center Willis Reed came flying toward us after he was tripped driving to the basket, stumbling right next to me, his sweat hitting the sleeve of my shirt. I was at once thrilled and terrified and Dad said, "Whadiya think of that Arty!" his thick Bronx accent accentuated by the intensity of the moment.

Those were the times when I felt closest to Dad, and I think the times he felt the best about being a father to me.

That, and when we went fishing, an activity we enjoyed together throughout most of our lives.

Dad would talk Yiddish to the fish, banter with the other people fishing, befriend Captain Ron and grin from ear to ear when I caught a fish, saying, "Ron, that's Arty's!" From the time I was around ten years old, our party fishing boat of choice was *The Fisherman,* owned by Ron Santee and sailing out of the Atlantic Highlands, N.J.

Captain Ron and Paul would create a bond that would last thirty years and include my mother, me and Santee's son, Ron Jr., the current owner and captain of the boat. Ron's wife, Rosemary, would become part of the friendship, as well. The Santees and Friedmans would socialize outside of fishing and the Santees would be invited and attend my wedding.

Dad would always wear his *"The Fisherman"* fishing cap and at one point became the supplier for the boat's spirit wear, the apparel retailer in him doing its thing. Mom also had a baseball jacket custom made for him with the words "Pinya the Fisherman" printed in bold letters across the back, an homage to her mother's nickname of "Pinya the Bluffer" for him.

Then there was the time that our friend Neil Wolf joined us for an early morning trip down the Garden State Parkway for a day of fishing, but we were late and missed the boat. So, Neil talked us into renting a skiff, buying some clams for bait and fishing for blowfish in Sandy Hook Bay.

It was a blast. We were out there for several hours, catching about a hundred fish – Neil called them "chicken of the sea" for their taste – that puffed up when we tried to unhook them. Back on shore, Neil and Dad scaled and fileted them until their hands could handle no more.

For Dad, fishing wiped away the tensions that were always inside him. It was athletic, even when for a big fish he had to hand over the rod to me or Mom or a mate on the boat because he felt chest pains coming on. He also loved the camaraderie of the boat crew and others on board.

He also never got seasick. One time in Florida, Dad and I went fishing even though we found out later there were small craft warnings for rough seas and that we never should have gone out. Within the first hour, Dad and I had caught some tarpon and snappers and had a snack, while everyone else on the boat was sick. The captain then called "all rods up" and headed back to the dock and refunded everyone their money.

"You guys sure have some sea legs," the captain said. Dad and I just laughed and said, "I guess we do."

During the Great Eastern days, Paul kept an office at the Little Falls store that was ten minutes from home. He would often invite me to come with him on Saturday mornings and give me a few dollars to play on the pinball machines and have a snack while he put in a couple of hours at the office or walking around the store. We would also sometimes make a trip to one of the other stores, providing camaraderie and togetherness.

Thanks to his job at Great Eastern, Mona and I also got to experience some Christmas magic during those years, even though we were Jewish and didn't celebrate the holiday.

That's because Paul would work late on Christmas Eve in the store helping out on the floor, usually at the Little Falls location. When the store closed, employees were allowed to purchase what was left in stock at a large discount, and Dad, in addition to some things he might have put aside during the day, would bring home a haul of toys, clothes and other goodies for the entire family.

He was so thrilled to do so, just like the thrill he and I both received when he would show up at the last minute at one of my Little League baseball games and the manager would ask him to coach one of the bases. He'd toss off his suit jacket and tie and jump on the field with the loudest voice cheering and coaching up my team at Maplewood Park.

When I got hit in the head with a pitch, he was the first one on the field. My ear was red for a week, but Dad was proud his son took it like a man, shedding no tears and wanting to stay in the game. When I made an All-Star team one year and made an over-the-shoulder catch of a fly ball in deep left center field, I heard his voice: "Great catch Arty, whoooo!"

THE CJC AND
A BAR MITZVAH

In 1961, Paul and Claire joined the Clifton Jewish Center, the local synagogue that would become the family's home away from home for many years.

Their reasons for doing so were many. First, Rabbi Markovitz rang our doorbell with a member of the temple to welcome us to town and ask us to join. Second, Grandpa Joe wanted a place to attend Saturday morning Shabbat services, being a religious man brought up in that tradition.

And third, it was time for me to start going to Sunday School. Mona didn't attend because at the time few girls her age did so. However, just a few years later, my Hebrew classes included as many girls as boys.

I often thought it was a mistake for my parents not to have Mona attend. They did give her a choice and she chose not to, but it may have caused a small rift between us and a feeling later on of being left out.

As they joined and became more involved in social and organizational temple affairs, Paul and Claire began to befriend couples who would become long-time or life-long

Arthur Friedman 03-31-1968

friends, especially the Levines. There were also the Bedrins, Wolfs, Levensteins and Gochmans, among many others, with whom Paul and Claire would socialize at the CJC services and affairs, as well as dinners out and at their houses, and significant family events.

But it was with the Levines – Jackie and Sunny and their children, Joyce and Elliot – that the most special and longest-lasting relationships existed. I am still close friends with Joyce and Elliot. The couples and their children would blend organically, with the women, Claire and Jackie, and the men, Paul and Sunny, bonding over family, social groups, sports and charitable endeavors.

Interestingly, Claire and Sunny were the easygoing, laid-back personalities in the mix, while Paul and Jackie were the outgoing, sometimes volatile types. The personality mix gave a balance to their friendships and marriage, and among the two couples proved to be dynamic, warm and loving, and made them and their families nearly inseparable.

Paul and Sunny joined the Men's Club and the Board of Directors of the CJC, while Claire and Jackie became active in the Sisterhood and the Jewish American ORT (Organization for Rehabilitation through Training) association that met at the temple.

Mona and I were thrown together with the Levines' children without protest and with long-lasting love and kinship. Joyce and I were the same age and in the same Sunday and Hebrew School classes. Later, we were in the same grade, school and classes in Woodrow Wilson Junior High School and Clifton High School.

When old enough, the four of us often spent evenings together watching TV and eating ice cream and cake and enjoying each

Arthur and Paul Friedman 1968

     Arthur Friedman

other's company. Joyce and I built a close personal bond and spent a lot of time together. This often resulted in us being teased by our friends about being romantically involved, which we weren't. Eventually, we would just tell people that we were cousins, which later would be true.

Joyce would say Mona became her role model socially, fashionably and in general demeanor, and Joyce would become the little sister Mona didn't have. Elliot and I shared a love of sports and games, and he was also a younger brother type to me. He also allowed me to not always be the youngest one in a social setting, since I was one of the youngest in my larger family circle. We spent a lot of time together, and Joyce and I still do.

That's because I reunited with John Stern at my 25th high school reunion. I told him the story of how I met my wife, Ellen, on a blind date set up by Jackie through her first cousin, Sonny Rogoff, Ellen's father. John and Joyce had just been divorced and both shared a mutual interest in seeing each other. I set it up and they were married a little over a year later.

Meanwhile, Dad and Sunny quickly rose up the ranks on the CJC board to vice presidents. Paul was vice president of Ways & Means, meaning he was in charge of fundraising, and he took to it with great zeal. Using his garment industry contacts and good will, he created and built up the synagogue's annual merchandise Bazaar to a $100,000 bonanza, and its yearly Tricky Tray into a huge success that was something close to it.

Paul would even draw in temple members Leo Nadel and Moe Sternberg, who also worked for him at Great Eastern, to run the events like a busy day at the store. Sunny, a textile executive who was also a former radio personality, would be on the microphone when he could get it out of Paul's hands. At the same time, Jackie and Claire would be working hard on the floor – Claire in her friendly, coercing way and Jackie somewhat more aggressively.

The days or evenings were often followed by a laugh-filled dinner or late-night snack at the Bonfire Restaurant or Tick Tock Diner, or take-out from the Village Deli. I personally had lots of fun being part of the festivities themselves, bringing home some goodies and enjoying the camaraderie between the families.

Paul rose to president of the Clifton Jewish Center in 1970 during a period of growth in both the general Jewish population and in temple membership. Like many large charitable organizations, problems and factions arose among the volunteer leadership.

Much stress surrounded an effort to replace one of the long-standing rabbis with someone more modern. Rabbi Markovitz was a founder of the CJC and contributed greatly to its growth and reputation in the town. He became chaplain of the Police and Fire Departments and helped start an interfaith program with other religious leaders in Clifton.

However, Markovitz was raised an Orthodox Jew and stuck to many of those beliefs and rules. This went against the established egalitarian tenet of the Conservative Judaism movement and threatened the growth of the CJC in the enlightened times of the 1960s.

Two factions developed at the temple – one that held deep respect for Markovitz, and one that felt it was time for a new, younger and more progressive rabbi to lead the congregation. Paul, a vice president at the time, did not want to oust the rabbi, but also didn't want to alienate or lose the members that wanted change.

Both sides had members that were influential, were strong financial benefactors and held board positions. It came down to a crucial general membership meeting where a vote was taken to determine whether the rabbi would be retained.

As Paul relayed afterward, impassioned speeches were given on both sides, including an inflammatory one in which one member, a Holocaust survivor who retained his thick Yiddish accent said of the attempted ouster, "That's how they did it in Russia!" referring to the Russian Revolution, in which Communists overthrew the ruling aristocracy.

This hyperbole enraged many, but a vote was taken in favor of Markovitz. Paul, Sunny Levine and Murry Bedrin tried to act as peacemakers, but generally to no avail. Some of the anti-Markovitz coalition left the CJC, while others stayed but became less active and donated fewer funds. It could be looked at as the beginning of the slow degradation of the temple's standing and size.

It wasn't until a generation later when I was a vice president of the CJC, with three daughters and a progressive mindset, that I introduced a motion to change the constitution to become an egalitarian congregation, giving girls and women equal standing in the religious ceremonies.

After the change was easily ratified, Markovitz came up to me a few days later and said, "That was a good thing you did for the temple. While I could never agree to it because it wasn't how I was brought up, it is the right way to go for the future of the temple."

When I became CJC president a year later, following in my father's footsteps, we did have a small membership boom that would not have occurred without the change in status. Fittingly, my mother and Shirley Kleinberg, who had seconded my motion and succeeded me as president, were the first two women to hold a *Torah* at the CJC in its history.

Paul also became involved in local Clifton community organizations and politics. He befriended Angelo Cupo, a builder who owned a construction company and was active and influential in town.

Paul joined the Optimists Club, a charitable organization whose members included many bigwigs in town. He was appointed to the City Traffic Board and helped push for more stop signs and lights for public safety in the burgeoning city. He also helped campaign for Cupo's nephew Tommy when he was elected to the City Council.

Wanting to put up a small basketball court and general athletic area in our backyard, Paul hired Cupo's construction company to do the job. The challenge was to get the concrete poured and laid deep into the yard. Cupo came up with the idea to run the concrete down the hill that led to the yard from the exit ramp that led from the Garden State Parkway to State Highway Route 3.

The problem was it blocked traffic and the cars started to back up. A Clifton Police car backed down the ramp and went to talk to the concrete truck crew. As Dad told me later, the cop was told the Cupo truck had permission and that he should speak to his chief. The chief evidently called the mayor and the policeman just drove away. The concrete was poured and the truck left, with about fifty cars following.

It was another case of Paul's mantra of "walk in the room like you own the place." Or the classic "it's not what you know, but who you know."

In a similar vein to his relationship with Danny Madison, Paul's friendship with Cupo extended from a business relationship to a personal one. When Cupo had heart surgery, Paul and Claire paid him a get-well visit at his home to find a line out the door comprised of family, friends, political allies and the like. After winding their way through the line of people as Dad said, "waiting to kiss his ring," Cupo spotted Claire and Paul and stood up and walked their way to greet them.

Calling them into an area where close family was breaking bread, Cupo, a tall, tanned figure, embraced them and said, "you don't wait on line, you're family."

On March 31, 1968, four days before my thirteenth birthday, I had my bar mitzvah. The congregation at the CJC was packed with my huge family at the time, including eighteen aunts and uncles and various cousins, Grandpa Joe and Grandma Monya, my parents' pack of friends from Clifton, Bayside and the Bronx, my friends and, of course, Mom, Dad and Mona.

That evening, my parents threw me a lavish party at the Chateau Renaissance in North Bergen that equaled many a wedding. We had about 250 people in a grand ballroom with a large dance floor and extraordinary full band.

I was at the center of a dais table flanked by Joyce on one side and my so-called girlfriend, Jeannie Schmidt, on the other. My friends, especially the non-Jewish ones who had never before seen a no-holds-barred bar mitzvah, were impressed and in awe.

My mother was happy with glee, my father was in his glory playing the big man on campus, and my grandfather just smiled from early in the morning when he belted out his alia (blessing over the *Torah*) as the Levite, to late at night seeing his only grandson become a man. Grandpa was to pass away eleven months later, but at that moment he seemed to be a self-fulfilled man.

The lavish evening included "enough food to feed an army," Claire said, including Chateau Briand steak as the main course and one of the biggest Viennese tables I've ever seen. It ended with the Sunday morning *Daily News* with the headline "Johnson Won't Run for a Second Term as President."

An incident involving the Vietnam War – the reason Johnson didn't seek re-election – proved to be an epiphany for Paul. That summer at the Democratic Convention in Chicago, the anti-war protestors clashed with Chicago police. This came after Mayor Richard Daly converted police vehicles into tanks to chase away protestors who had just erected a Vietnamese flag atop a flagpole in front of the Convention Center.

Historians have dubbed what followed a "police riot," as protestors were clubbed, bloodied and arrested while inside chaos broke out between Daley forces and party officials.

Sitting at home in front of the TV, the Friedman family was divided. Mona, now seventeen and with friends involved in the Anti-war Movement and enrolled in ROTC; me, starting to get nervous about if I would have to be drafted and go off to war; Dad, acting patriotic and yelling at the protestors, and Mom, taking it all in.

"Hit them in the head, the head!" Paul said emotionally.

"But Paul, those could be your kids," Mom said thoughtfully.

Dad got very quiet for a couple of minutes, taking in what his wife had said. Then tears started streaming down his face and he started sobbing.

"Leave them alone, you bastards," he shouted toward the cops on the screen.

In that instant, Paul had switched from a patriotic citizen to a concerned parent against the war. By the time I was seventeen and received my draft card and draft lottery number, Dad had created a situation for me to go to work and live in Montreal, Canada, setting me up with a potential job at a textile factory through a business contact of his. He wasn't sending his son off to fight and possibly get killed in an unjustified war.

Fortunately, the war ended in November 1972 for the United States when President Richard Nixon pulled the last troops out of Saigon. Otherwise, in June 1973 when I graduated from Clifton High School, I would have been eligible to be drafted.

Arthur and Paul Friedman 1969

VACATION TIME

During Mona's and my youth and teen years, we were fortunate to go with our parents and some extended family on many family vacations. One memorable one was to the Los Angeles area, where we had many cousins on Paul and Claire's side of the family. Joining us was Grandpa Joe and cousin Felice.

We were greeted with a lavish barbecue at the home of Leo and Florence Presser, and Mona and I became fast friends with their children Jeff, Steve and Marilyn. My parents were able to invite anyone they wanted and cousins from the area arrived in throngs.

My cousin Elaine, daughter of Florence's sister, Thelma, and her husband Saul, joined the circle we formed with the Presser children. This group of cousins visited each other often on either coast in the coming years. Grandpa Joe even bonded with Thelma and Florence's father, Bennie, discovering that they were from the same town in Poland before they emigrated to New York in their teens.

A couple of memorable stories Paul liked to tell stemmed from family trips to Los Angeles. Among the tales were when he visited his Aunt Dora, Monya's sister, who had lost her son, Frankie, in his early adulthood. We went for a Sunday dinner where Dora lived with her daughter, son-in-law and grandchildren, and when Paul walked in to see Dora for the first time in many years, Dora said something like, "How can that be Frankie?" and basically fainted.

Then Dad said, "No Aunt Dora, it's me, your nephew Pinny, Paul, Monya's son." Dora said, "You look so much liked Frankie, oh my God!" They cried and hugged and kissed for a while, and then all was OK.

During a vacation a few years later, my cousin Felice came with us, and we spent one of the days at Disneyland. Felice spent a lot of time with our family during her teens and early adulthood years as a respite from living in an apartment in the Bronx with her parents, Sophie and Harry.

Felice must have been around twenty or twenty-one years old, and very beautiful, during the trip. One sunny day we went to the first Disney theme park. She and Paul apparently were walking down Main Street together at one point and were seen but not approached by one of Dad's business associates.

When Paul returned home and went back to work, he was at a business meeting and the acquaintance said, "Hey Paul, that was some beautiful blond you were with at Disneyland!"

"What are you talking about?" Dad told us he said to the man when relaying the story that night. "Oh, that must have been my niece, who came with our family on our vacation. My wife and kids were right there with us, schmuck!"

They had a good laugh about it and gave Felice the chance to refer to herself as the "beautiful blond" when reminded of the story.

Several family vacations during this period also included car trips to Cape Cod, where I believe Dad first started talking to the fish in the ocean, urging them to come on to his hook and line.

We would all go on these party boats for a half-day of fishing, sightseeing and family bonding. Paul was in his glory kibitzing with the mates and others on the boat, as well as with me, Mona and Mom.

Then he would start talking in Yiddish to the fish, with sayings like, "Come on, you *momzer*," meaning a smart-aleck or bastard. Or, he would refer to them as his *kindila*, or little children. He got some funny looks from others on the boat, comments from Mona like, "What are you doing, it's so embarrassing." Mom and I would generally just laugh and shake our heads. What he was doing was having a good time and relaxing and relieving stress.

In the early days, Grandpa Joe joined us on at least one trip, and this is also where I remember Dad and Grandpa's routine of who would pay for dinner. "You paying tonight Yussel (or Joe or Pop)?" Pinny would ask, to which Grandpa would reply, "You can't scare me!" Let's just say Dad always paid for dinner.

It was on these trips where Claire, Mona and I all learned to eat seafood like lobster, crab and shrimp, since we never ate them at home. Claire had actually never even tried lobster until she was in her late thirties, having grown up in a kosher home. Cape Cod always had the best seafood restaurants, and we all learned to love the food there.

I think those vacations were the best times for Paul. He was able to forget the stress and toil of the job and the past that haunted him inwardly. It was full-time family fun and bonding and he never seemed happier.

Dad would literally burst into song – he had a pretty good voice – hug and kiss Claire in public and buy his children anything they wanted while planting his signature wet kisses on us randomly. This was the warm and fuzzy side of Pinny that was at odds with a darker side of anger, rage and depression that would sometimes overtake his personality.

Claire and Paul Friedman 1990

CAREER AND HEALTH CRISIS

Great Eastern had been acquired by Diana Stores in 1962, and when it was sold to Daylin Corporation in 1969, it was the end of an era for the Schneiders and for Paul.

In 1970, he left to become vice president and general merchandise manager of M.H. Fishman department stores. He held the same title at Volume Merchandising from 1972 to 1975, and then went to I.M. Burt Stores, where he was general merchandise manager from 1975 to 1978.

Fishman and Volume, both based in New York City, operated chains of mid-sized discount specialty stores across the country. Burt, based in Irvington, New Jersey, was a chain of moderately-priced women's apparel stores in New Jersey.

It was during this time that Paul suffered a series of physical and mental setbacks. During one of his business trips while working for Volume Merchandising, I accompanied Dad on a jaunt to Texas. We were both shocked at all the gun racks in the pickup trucks, the intense heat and the sheer size of the state as we drove from San Antonio to El Paso.

In El Paso, I hooked up with my friend Steve Seigel, who was in the army at the time and based in Fort Bliss. It was here that Dad had an unquenchable thirst, asking me to keep getting him drinks. When we got home, he discovered he had diabetes. He went on medication and a Weight Watchers diet and lost 80 pounds but still had diabetes.

Before that, around 1967, Dad broke his knee cap. While playing touch football in front of our house on Huemmer Terrace during a BBQ with business associates, family and friends, he jumped for a ball and hit a car parked on the street. Apparently, the competitive athlete still laid within him.

A few years later, while vacationing in Florida and walking at poolside, the knee collapsed, leaving Paul with a limp the rest of his life. We had to cut short the vacation and somehow were allowed to fly home on a plane to New Jersey.

Dad's old friend, Danny Madison, figured out a way to have a car meet us on the tarmac at Newark Airport and drive Dad straight to the hospital for another knee surgery. Yes, these were simpler times and that could probably never happen again, but how Danny Madison made those arrangements is a mystery to me because I was told not to ask questions. Madison also arranged to have the team doctor for the New York Giants at the time perform the surgery.

Around 1975, when Paul was about 48, he suffered his first heart attack. It followed several years of chest pains and taking angina medication to treat his ailment. He recovered but was told that he was not a candidate for bypass surgery, and that he should "move to Florida and try to live as long as he can."

This was not acceptable to Claire, who diligently pursued a second opinion. She found a young heart surgeon operating out of Valley Hospital in Ridgewood, New Jersey, who said Paul was clearly a candidate for bypass surgery. He performed the quadruple bypass on his coronary arteries, with a recovery that lasted 10 years.

During this time, amid the end of his tenure at Great Eastern and going through the trauma of the knee and heart surgeries, Paul slipped into a moderate clinical depression. His normal outgoing, loud and vivacious personality was inhibited, and fortunately for him, Claire and Dr. Handler, his primary care doctor, diagnosed it and had him begin to see a psychiatrist, Dr. Morrow.

Paul's therapy sessions brought out childhood traumatic experiences that had been repressed for decades. These included the horrific time his father, Aaron, had forced him to say *Kaddish* (the Prayer for the dead) for his sister Ruthie because she had married a non-Jewish man without her parents' permission.

The therapy also allowed Paul to express the troubled childhood he had endured. Being an adolescent during the Great Depression, he often went without adequate food, clothing or basic necessities of life. These brought on insecurities and feelings of inferiority and despair.

Worst of all, this period of Paul's life was dominated by parents who were too incapable, unwilling, and uneducated to offer him the emotional support and childhood training to deal with life's challenges. Dad would reveal to his psychiatrist and family the way Aaron and Monya would use anger and fear to discipline their children, and how that led to Paul and his siblings feeling alienated and developing a distorted sense of self-worth.

Dad would say it wasn't until he went to high school that he was able to find an outlet for his emotions through friendships, as well as a use for his athletic ability to build self-esteem. When he met and became serious with Claire, he truly developed his real personality and was able to realize his true self-actualization.

Dad was helped through his depression by his great friend, Sunny Levine, who would come to the house and mainly just listen, but also talk quietly about sports, the Clifton Jewish Center and life in general. His kindness and friendship, along with the therapy sessions and new hobbies like painting slowly drew Paul out of his depression.

While Paul had a large family with two brothers and three sisters, it was people like Sam Tolkoff and Sunny Levine who would be his closest allies in life. They carried no emotional baggage from the difficult childhood he endured and had the combination of friendship and personal bond he yearned.

It was also why in many ways Paul became closer to Claire's family than his own over the years, particularly the Hanigs and Donenfelds, the families of Claire's sisters, Helen and Sophie. Their husbands, Sam and Harry, weren't exactly his best friends, but a closeness and familiarity built up. But their daughters, Carol and Felice, adored Uncle Paul and Aunt Claire and we spent much time with them growing up.

While working at Burt, Paul and Claire opened what would become a six-store chain of women's specialty boutiques in northern New Jersey called Monette's. Named after Mona, the store had Mom at the operational helm and Dad doing the buying.

They were joined by Moe Sternberger and Leo Nadel, who had worked for Paul at Great Eastern, to help run the business, while Leo's wife, Lil, managed the flagship store in Richfield Village in Clifton. I also worked there a couple of summers while I was in college, making deliveries.

Monette's was actually a success and achieved popularity, but it probably expanded too much and too quickly, and was hurt by the recession of 1981. The chain closed shortly thereafter, leaving Paul and Claire in financial hardship as they used some of their own funds to pay for the expansion and lost most of it in bankruptcy.

In 1978, at the age of fifty-one, Dad had made a switch to wholesale, becoming a purchasing agent for Ben Elias Industries, a large sportswear jobber in Manhattan's Garment District. Paul had purchased merchandise from Ben Elias for many years and had built a professional and personal relationship with Butch and Stanley Elias, two brothers who now owned the business.

The job gave Dad a new lease on his career, and Mom started working for the company as well, as a store manager for its outlet store in Moonachie, New Jersey, and later on Long Island. The job allowed Paul to make deals and meet with people on a regular basis and feel vital again.

Unfortunately, about ten years after his first heart attack, Paul had another one. At age fifty-eight, he recovered again and continued to work until he finished his career at Elias, retiring in 1990.

Shortly before he retired, I began working as a market editor at *Women's Wear Daily* in New York. My first front page story and byline was in November 1989, a feature about how wool coats had not been selling well due to warm weather and a new generation of jackets made from performance fabrics.

Dad came home and called me on the phone to tell me a story.

"I went into a showroom and the man I was to meet had his *Women's Wear Daily* out on the table," Dad said. "It had your byline on it and he said, 'Hey Friedman, you know this guy?' I said, 'Yes, that's my son!' You made me proud Arty!'"

Claire, Arthur, and Paul Friedman 1990

A LEGACY

I do think that Paul's greatest achievement – more important than his high school sports accolades, his success as a business executive and leader and president of the Clifton Jewish Center – was as a father.

He was far from perfect, we'll leave that near-title to Claire, but he gave a strong effort from the heart despite having to work long hours as Mona and I were growing up. I remember him many times rushing to my Little League baseball games with his suit on just in time to throw off his jacket and tie and coach third base, which put a big smile on my face.

There was also sponge ball practice in front of the house, where even when Paul got overweight or had a limp from his knee surgery, he could still hit and throw the ball farther than his son or any other adults around. He would also shoot the basketball around our make-shift court in the backyard with me and some of my friends.

While he couldn't move around much anymore, his set shot distance still had uncanny accuracy, or as my friend Carl Jackameit would say, "Mr. Friedman can still shoot."

Dad also had a special relationship with Mona. He would do anything for her. When he looked at her it was nearly the same look he gave Mom. It was the look that said, despite his anger issues and less-nuanced parenting skills than his wife, Mona was always his *"Malka Shana,"* his beautiful girl.

Maybe the proudest I ever was of Dad was when Mona came to him to tell him she wanted to marry Louis Bucceri, an Italian Catholic young man she had been dating for several years. Louis was about to graduate from New York University Law School. When Mona and Mom told me what Dad said I was glad because I liked Lou and saw how happy he made Mona.

When Dad was asked for his approval, there was fear among Mona and Mom that he would say intermarriage was forbidden under Jewish law, and that he couldn't approve. Instead, Paul told them, "I won't do what my father did to my sister and to me. The most important thing is that you're happy."

Like Uncle Teddy wrote about his father, Israel Kleiner, in *To Break the Barrier*, the laws of a religion, Jewish or Catholic, can and should be overcome by love and happiness, Dad declared. Mona and Lou were married in a lavish affair at the same venue as my bar mitzvah six years earlier, with a priest and rabbi presiding and Dad bursting with *nachas*.

When Mona and Lou had three young children – Jennifer, Laura and Andrew – Paul actually dressed up as Santa Claus and surprised them on Christmas morning. This was completely unexpected for me to hear, but his joy at being a grandfather who adored his grandchildren towered above all. He was also a great Santa Claus in his store-bought outfit and his loud "Ho, ho, ho!"

Unfortunately, he was already stricken with Parkinson's Disease when my two older daughters were born. The result was that neither of them, nor my wife, Ellen, whom I married in 1990, got to know the real Paul Friedman.

The Dad I remember was the man Paul with the vivacious personality who could light up a room. He was the Pinny with the quick wit who could make everyone in the room laugh. Dad was also the person I admired for his interests, from sports to religion, and most importantly, his love of his family.

On Ellen and my wedding video, Dad forewent the usually gushy superlatives and said, "I love you kids and may you have a long life full of happiness and love, and may the Yankees, Knicks, Rangers and Giants all win the championship this year! And if you believe that, I'll tell you another one!"

Before Dad retired at age sixty-five in 1992, he and Mom had purchased a condominium in Pompano Beach, Florida, where they planned to live in the winter months and where Dad could pursue his beloved hobby of fishing. When Ellen and I and our newborn baby, Heather, went to visit them that first winter in 1993, Dad wasn't feeling well and was in bed with an unknown ailment. Shortly thereafter, he was diagnosed with Parkinson's Disease and came back to New Jersey for treatment.

Like the strong athlete that he was, he staged a comeback for a while. He and Mom were even able to attend and enjoy their 50th Wedding Anniversary party in December 1996. He then took a turn for the worse and was mostly confined to a wheelchair as his heart muscle got weaker.

I remember sitting with him watching a Yankees game as my one-year-old daughter Karen crawled up to see him and he smiled and threw her a kiss.

"Arty, what am I going to do?" Dad asked. "What's going to be?"

Knowing there was no cure and his health was failing, all I could say was, "You're going to take each day as it comes. You taught me that life isn't always fair and like the Yankees, you have to play with the lineup you're given."

"I guess you're right, Arty. I love you, you know," he said.

"I love you too, Dad," I answered.

Paul Friedman passed away on June 13, 1997, at the age of sixty-nine, two days before Father's Day and a month short of his seventieth birthday. His funeral was held that Sunday, ironically on Father's Day, and was attended by hundreds of people. Family, friends and business associates came from all over.

In came childhood friends Sammy Tolkoff and Jonesy, and dear friends made at the Clifton Jewish Center. There were also beloved siblings, nieces and nephews, children and grandchildren. Of course, his children were also there, as well as the love of his life for more than 55 years, Claire. Eulogies were given by Rabbi Eugene Markovitz, Paul's rabbi at the CJC for thirty-five years, and by "the two Arthurs," as Joyce (Levine) Stern called us: Dad's best friend Arthur "Sunny" Levine, and me.

We told of his love of family, sports, religion, humor and his larger-than-life personality. We didn't mention his faults or troubles, but focused on the Paul Friedman that was loved by so many.

Sunny talked about the laughter the two men shared, the bond they had created and the times they spent together. "I'll miss you Pinny," he ended, and I know he did.

I talked about Dad's love of sports and his teams. One story I shared was when the famous Bucky Dent home run was hit at Fenway Park in 1978. Dad had to step out and walk around the block to ward off excitement-induced chest pains brought on by the winner-take-all game that *Rosh Hashana.*

I said how Steve Seigel used to call our house "Sports Center" before the ESPN show ever came into existence.

I ended with a nod to baseball and the great film *Field of Dreams* that had come out in 1989 and which I made Dad watch with me. Fortunately for me, I said, unlike the characters, the Kinsellas, in the movie, my dad and I had a relationship and reveled in enjoying and playing sports together.

In the film, Ray Kinsella is given the opportunity to have the game of catch with his dad that never happened in real life.

"Thanks for playing catch with me, Dad," I said in my conclusion.

I know when Paul Friedman entered Heaven, he walked in like he owned the place.

Dad's legacy and memory live on in many intangible and tangible ways. Nobody who knew him will ever forget him, because as his posthumous song for my oldest daughter Heather's bat mitzvah noted, he was "Unforgettable."

Just before Sammy Tolkoff's death in 2020, I was able to reconnect with his daughter, Marcy, and talk about Sam's influence on Paul and how much my parents adored Sam. Marcy then relayed that to Sam, and she told me that her father, who wasn't very well and hadn't been talking much, perked up when he heard Paul Friedman's name and reminisced for forty-five minutes.

"I was so happy and surprised," she said. "It was clear how much he loved Paul and the great friendship they had."

Lastly and maybe most poignantly, my youngest daughter, Rebecca Paige, or in Hebrew, *Penina Rasel,* is named after her grandfather who she never met. Rebecca shares his flamboyance, knack for sports and has been told to tackle new challenges in life by taking them on like you own them.

ABOUT THE AUTHOR

This is the first novella for Arthur Friedman. His career was spent primarily in journalism, where after thirty-five years, he retired in 2022.

Arthur got his start at *Wayne Today* as a freelancer covering high school sports. He

Author Arthur Friedman

was then able to get a full-time job as a reporter at the *Ridgewood News*, where he received hands-on experience and training as a reporter and editor in a fast-paced, exciting environment under the mentorship of Lorraine Mullica Ash and Diana Bucco St. Lifer.

Arthur learned to write on deadline, construct concise stories with crisp leads covering municipal government, local politics, entrepreneurs and personalities. He interviewed chiefs of police, mayors and state and Congressional representatives, and had the great opportunity to meet and interview Harrison Ford, one of his favorite actors.

Thanks to that great experience, Arthur was able to then begin a thirty-three-year stint as a reporter and editor covering the world of fashion and international trade at *Women's Wear Daily* and *Sourcing Journal*. He was able to meet and interview a great variety of people during this time.

Some of his favorites were Katie Couric, Marilu Henner, Oscar de la Renta, Bill Blass, Carolina Herrera, Stan Herman, Abe Schrader, Susan Lucci and Donna Karan. He also interviewed and befriended three of the nicest people he met in his life: Bud Konheim, Jeffry Aaronson and Tricia Carey.

Sourcing Journal rounded his career and Arthur credits its founder, Eddie Hertzman, and his own reputation proudly built up over more than three decades for extending his career for more than five years as senior editor at *SJ*.

Arthur, who earned his Bachelor of Arts degree from Fairleigh Dickinson University and Master of Arts degree in Social Sciences at Montclair State University, was also an adjunct history professor at Montclair State for 10 years and has continued his teaching as an English tutor, first at Huntington Learning Center and then at Sylvan Learning Center.

Arthur lives in Clifton, New Jersey, where he grew up, with his wife, Ellen, and their two cats, Layla and Skye. He is most proud of his three daughters, Heather, Karen and Rebecca.

ACKNOWLEDGMENTS

My inspiration for this book first and foremost came from Paul and Claire Friedman, and Mona Bucceri, my first nuclear family who I love eternally. They helped to give me a wonderful life, and their memories supplied much of the material for my endeavor to tell Dad's story.

I also owe debts of gratitude and encouragement to my second nuclear family: my wife Ellen, and daughters Heather, Karen and Rebecca. Karen, who would regularly ask when the book was going to be finished so she could read it, being as interested in family history and lore as me, also edited the book and designed the book cover.

Heather provided inspiration by taking her childhood dream of becoming a Doctor of Veterinary Medicine and making it a reality by whatever means it took. Rebecca gave me confidence by following in my journalistic footsteps and taking her namesake grandfather's name to heart and keeping his legacy alive through her own version of "walking into the place like you own it."

Ellen gave me confidence by never really doubting me, saying often to friends and family, "Arty is retiring and writing a book," and asking, "How's the book going?"

I also want to thank Lorraine Ash, my first editor in journalism and life-long friend, who offered me great advice, encouragement and confidence. Lorraine also recommended Sherry Wachter, my project manager for this book, who offered professionalism, experience and a guiding light to follow.

Then there are people like Joyce and John Stern, Paul Dreifuss, Eric Hertzman, Vicki M. Young, Tricia Carey and Jill Rosenberg who uplifted me by showing confidence in my ability to complete the task and through their friendship and love.

Arthur Friedman